Prepositions

over

between

in

around

behind

along

with

by Ann Heinrichs

[Content Adviser: Kathy Rzany, M.A., Adjunct Professor,
School of Education, Dominican University, River Forest, Illinois]

Published by The Child's World®
1980 Lookout Drive • Mankato, MN 56003-1705
800-599-READ • www.childsworld.com

Cover and page 1: JIANG HONGYAN/Shutterstock.com; 5: Vadim.Petrov/
Shutterstock.com; 7: Chalermpon Poungpeth/Shutterstock.com; 9: Golden Pixels
LLC/Shutterstock.com; 10: © Monkey Business Images/Dreamstime.com; 13:
Rusty Dodson/Shutterstock.com; 15: klevers/Shutterstock.com; 17: Jon Nicholls
Photography/Shutterstock.com; 19: Talvi/Shutterstock.com; 21: Jeka/Shutterstock
.com; 23: PosiNote/Shutterstock.com; 25: DenisProduction.com/Shutterstock.com;
27: © Petro/Dreamstime.com; 29: © Ulianna19970/Dreamstime.com

ISBN: 9781503832442
LCCN: 2018957538

Printed in the United States of America
PA02423

ABOUT THE AUTHOR

Ann Heinrichs is the author of more than 200 books for children
and young adults. She has also enjoyed successful careers as a
children's book editor and an advertising copywriter. Ann grew
up in Fort Smith, Arkansas, and now lives in Chicago, Illinois.

Contents

CHAPTER ONE

What Is a Preposition?

[

Definition: A preposition is a word that links another word or group of words to other parts of the sentence. Prepositions introduce a description or a relationship such as time or place.

]

EXAMPLES

In the morning, Skipper runs **between** the rows **of** apple trees **along** the edge **of** the park.

All the orange words in the sentence above are prepositions. Like glue, they connect words with one another. As you see, many prepositions are tiny words—**in, on, of, at,** and **by.** Others are much longer, such as **between, outside, underneath,** and **throughout.**

Imagine what fun a dog would have running **between** the rows **of** apple trees **in** this orchard! You would use three prepositions to tell about it—between, of, and in.

What would you do without prepositions? You'd have trouble saying anything at all! Prepositions (the orange and blue words below) can help you point out a time or a place.

EXAMPLES

TIME	PLACE
on Tuesday	**on** the chair
in 2020	**in** school
at noon	**at** the library
by three o'clock	**by** the benches
around midnight	**around** the corner
between classes	**between** your eyes

Prepositions can also help you describe something.

EXAMPLES
the clown **with** the blue nose
cookies **for** sale
a longhorn steer **from** Texas

Rule: Every preposition has an object.

A preposition never stands alone. It's always followed by an object. The object of the preposition is usually a noun or a pronoun. Sometimes, however, the object is an adverb.
Look at the examples below. The orange words are objects of prepositions. Can you name the prepositions?

EXAMPLES

NOUN	Put the hamster's cage behind the **couch.**
PRONOUN	This story was written about **me.**
PRONOUN	This trophy belongs to **her.**
ADVERB	I've been confused until **now.**

The basketball is about to go through the hoop. You need the preposition through to introduce the place where the basketball is going.

NOW TRY THESE!

In these sentences, pick out the preposition and the object of the preposition. Then tell whether the preposition introduces a time, a place, or a description.

1. Where are my socks with the blue toes?
2. Tomorrow Daniel will get up at five o'clock.
3. Why can't Amanda play beside the lake?
4. Make sure the basketball goes through the hoop.

See page 32 for the answers. Don't peek!

CHAPTER TWO

Prepositional Phrases

[
Definition: A prepositional phrase =
the preposition + its object + all
the words that modify the object.
]

A prepositional phrase is a little bundle of information. It consists of the preposition and its object, along with all the words that modify the object. The preposition is like a hook. It hooks the whole phrase to whatever word the phrase modifies. The phrase might be acting as an adjective or an adverb. It all depends on which word the phrase modifies.

[
Rule: A prepositional phrase acts
as an adjective when it modifies
a noun or pronoun. It acts as
an adverb when it modifies a
verb, adjective, or other adverb.
]

You could use lots of prepositional phrases to describe these girls. Some examples are in the pool, on their faces, over their eyes, under the water, and with their legs. Can you say sentences about the girls using these prepositional phrases?

Many grandchildren love hearing the life stories of their grandparents. In this sentence, of their grandparents is a prepositional phrase modifying the noun stories.

Look at the prepositional phrases below. They are all acting as adjectives. That's because they all modify nouns. In each example, name the noun that is modified by the prepositional phrase.

EXAMPLES

I love hearing the life story of my Grandma.
The bunny with the floppy ears is my favorite.
Let's meet at the store on the corner of State and Main.

Now look at the prepositional phrases at the top of page 11. They are acting as adverbs. Why? Because they modify verbs. They tell how, when, or where.

QUICK FACT

An adverb is a word that modifies a verb, an adjective, or another adverb. Adverbs often tell how, when, or where.

> **EXAMPLES**
>
> The twins swim **without fear.**
> I got here at **seven o'clock.**
> Lightning flashed **across the sky.**

When a prepositional phrase begins a sentence, it's usually followed by a comma.

> **EXAMPLES**
>
> **In the shadows,** a yellow bird appeared.
> **Across the marsh,** we heard the sounds of croaking frogs.
> **At sunset,** the guards lowered the flag.

Some words can be either a preposition or an adverb. What's your clue for which is which? It's a preposition if it has an object.

> **EXAMPLES**
>
> PREPOSITION — Stay **inside** the park.
> ADVERB — I'm going **inside.**
>
> PREPOSITION — Emma gazed **out** the window.
> ADVERB — The mouse scurried **out.**
>
> PREPOSITION — Brian crept **along** the wall.
> ADVERB — Three lions strolled **along.**

CHAPTER THREE

The Frog on the Log

> **EXAMPLES**
>
> There's a frog **on** a log **in** a hole
> **at** the bottom **of** the sea.

Sometimes it takes a lot of prepositional phrases to say what you mean! The sentence above tells just exactly where that frog is. Each preposition links its prepositional phrase to the word the phrase modifies.

> **EXAMPLES**
>
> | PREPOSITIONAL PHRASE | MODIFIES |
> | --- | --- |
> | on a log | is (from There is) |
> | in a hole | log |
> | at the bottom | hole |
> | of the sea | bottom |

Here's a frog on a log in a pond full of water plants. How many prepositions are in this sentence? If you guessed three, you're right!

NOW TRY THESE!

Write four sentences with lots of prepositional phrases. Use these words in your sentences:

1. cat – hat – head – bed
2. dog – frog – rose – nose
3. fish – dish – tail – pail
4. Jack – yak – sack – back

See page 32 for the answers. Don't peek!

CHAPTER FOUR

Get Rid of That Preposition!

Sometimes the words **and** and **or** join two or more prepositional phrases. If those phrases have the same preposition, you don't need to repeat it. Just get rid of it!

EXAMPLES

Sydney wears that hat **in** summer and ~~in~~ winter.
Give these scraps **to** the cat or ~~to~~ the dog.
I have valentines **for** Kayla, ~~for~~ John, and ~~for~~ Austin.

You see? Nothing is lost. The preposition simply has more than one object.

Sometimes people use two prepositions when one will do just fine. The extra preposition is not necessary at all. Just get rid of it!

EXAMPLES

The pie fell **off** ~~of~~ the windowsill.
Snoopy stayed **inside** ~~of~~ his doghouse.
My turtle crawled **out** ~~of~~ the door!

You don't need to say your cat took a nap inside of the box. Just say, "My cat took a nap inside the box!"

CHAPTER FIVE

Wait! I Need All These Prepositions!

You just learned not to use too many prepositions. Now change gears. Sometimes several words act together as a preposition. In this case, you can't do without those extra words.

EXAMPLES

He was **out of** control.
That song is **out of** sight.
I'll have peas **instead of** broccoli.
According to Bill, the party's over.

These two-word groups are considered prepositions. They work together as one. They have objects, and they connect prepositional phrases to the words they modify. There are even some three-word preposition groups:

EXAMPLES

in addition to	in regard to
on account of	in spite of

According to our friends, this girl is the best skateboarder in town. Her tricks are out of sight! In these sentences, the two-word groups according to and out of act together as one preposition.

CHAPTER SIX

Quick! Un-Dangle That Preposition!

[
Definition: A preposition at the end of a sentence is called a dangling preposition.
]

EXAMPLES

Which shoes are you looking **for?**
This is the best book I've ever come **across.**
Afghanistan is the subject I want to write **about.**
The elephant went back where it came **from.**

See the orange words in these examples? They're all prepositions. But where are their objects? The prepositions are hanging out there at the end of the sentence, just dangling in midair. That's why they're called dangling prepositions.

How is a dangling preposition like an elephant's tail? It's just dangling out there at the very end, with nothing coming after it.

Grammar experts disagree about dangling prepositions. Most experts agree on some points, though. Dangling prepositions may be all right for casual talking. However, it's best to avoid them in writing.

DID YOU KNOW?

Dangling prepositions were first "outlawed" in the 1600s. The English poet John Dryden declared them to be wrong. Today, some grammar experts say this rule is too old. They say we need dangling prepositions for clear communication. Others say dangling prepositions are a definite no-no!

How can you un-dangle a preposition? There's good news and bad news. First, here's the bad news. When a dangling preposition is corrected, the sentence sounds awkward. Here are the proper ways to say the sentences on page 18!

EXAMPLES
For which shoes are you looking?
This is the best book across which I've ever come.
Afghanistan is the subject about which I want to write.
The elephant went back to the place from which it came.

The good news is, there's a better way to fix dangling prepositions. Simply choose different words.

EXAMPLES
Which shoes do you want?
This is the best book I've ever read.
I want to write about Afghanistan.
The elephant went back to its home.

CHAPTER SEVEN

Such As . . . ?

Like is a tricky preposition. It sneaks into places where other words belong. Often you'll find **like** sneaking into places where **such as** belongs. Some simple rules will help you keep things straight.

Use **like** when you mean "similar to." Look at the examples at the top of page 22. Try putting "similar to" in place of **like.** You'll find that the meaning stays the same.

Her brother says she has crazy ideas. She says, "Such as?" because she wants examples. We use **such as** to introduce examples.

> **EXAMPLES**
> You look **like** a movie star!
> It all seemed **like** a dream.
> He felt **like** a fool.
> We need more teams **like** the White Sox.
> Nimbi ran **like** the wind.

Use **such as** when you're giving examples.

> **EXAMPLES**
>
> WRONG   I love rich colors **like** purple, gold, and red.
> RIGHT   I love rich colors **such as** purple, gold, and red.
>
> WRONG   Let's invite close friends **like** Tyler and Megan.
> RIGHT   Let's invite close friends **such as** Tyler and Megan.
>
> WRONG   Bring munchies **like** pretzels.
> RIGHT   Bring munchies **such as** pretzels.

These sentences are naming actual examples. That's why **such as** is correct. Remember—**like** means "similar to." You don't love colors *similar* to purple, gold, and red. You don't want to invite friends *similar* to Tyler and Megan. And you don't want munchies *similar* to pretzels. You want the real thing!

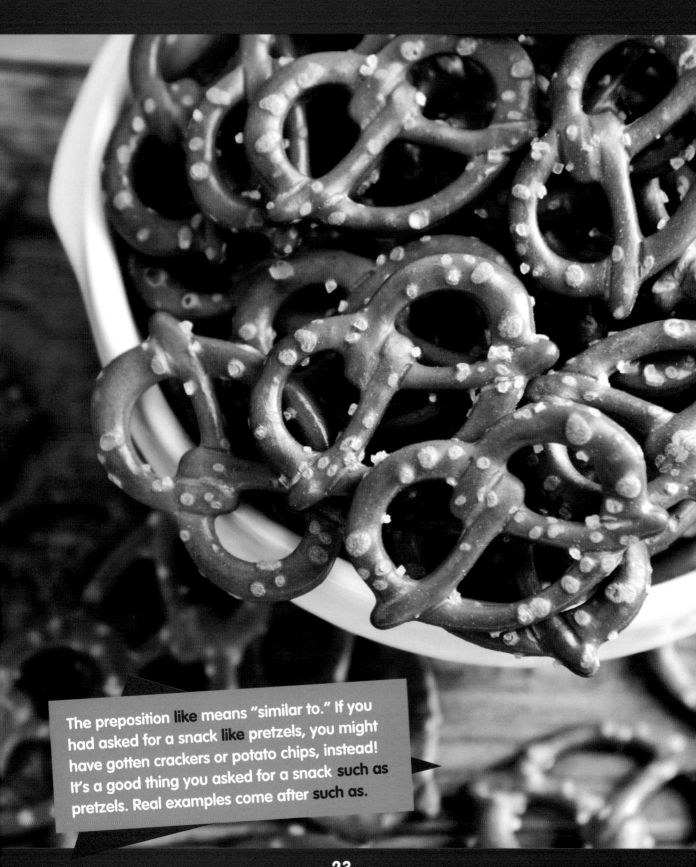

The preposition like means "similar to." If you had asked for a snack like pretzels, you might have gotten crackers or potato chips, instead! It's a good thing you asked for a snack such as pretzels. Real examples come after such as.

CHAPTER EIGHT

As If!

As you see, **like** is not only tricky. It's downright sneaky! You'll also find **like** sneaking into the place of **as if.** Again, just follow some simple rules for which words to use.

Like is a preposition. It's always followed by an object. **As if** is a conjunction. It joins two clauses, or complete thoughts.

> **Definition: A clause expresses a complete thought. It can stand alone and make sense. Every clause has a subject and a verb.**

In the following examples, **like** might seem to be correct. But it's not! **As if** is correct. Look at each group of words following **as if.** They are clauses. They express a complete thought, and they can stand alone.

EXAMPLES

WRONG	He played his trumpet **like** his life depended on it.
RIGHT	He played his trumpet **as if** his life depended on it.
WRONG	She screamed **like** the sheet really covered a ghost.
RIGHT	She screamed **as if** the sheet really covered a ghost.
WRONG	I felt **like** I would explode with joy!
RIGHT	I felt **as if** I would explode with joy!

"When I heard him play the trumpet, I felt as if I would explode with joy!" As if is a conjunction joining complete thoughts.

HOT TIP

The preposition like means "similar to." Like is never followed by a clause.

CHAPTER NINE

More Tricky Prepositions

Think you've learned it all? Here are more tricky prepositions to keep you busy!

Use **between** for two people or things. Use **among** for more than two.

EXAMPLES

RIGHT   Secret signals passed **between** David and Jacob.

RIGHT   She started a discussion **among** the kids in the class.

WRONG   She started a discussion **between** the kids in the class.

Use **beside** for a location. Use **besides** when you mean "other than."

EXAMPLES

RIGHT   I love to sit **beside** the lake.

RIGHT   No one showed up **besides** Jonathan.

WRONG   No one showed up **beside** Jonathan.

Use **more than** for a quantity of things that are being counted. Use **over** to show movement in a direction. But watch out! You also use **over** with a number that's *not* being counted one by one.

Jennifer and Jessica are relaxing **beside** the lake. There is no one around **besides** these two sisters.

EXAMPLES

RIGHT The hawk flew **over** the cuckoo's nest.

RIGHT We collected **more than** 20 coupons.

WRONG We collected **over** 20 coupons.

RIGHT This contest is for kids **over** nine years old.

Use **since** to show time that has passed. Use **because** only to connect two clauses.

EXAMPLES

RIGHT I've been waiting **since** Monday.

RIGHT We're all wet **because** it was raining.

WRONG We're all wet **since** it was raining.

CHAPTER TEN

Just between You and Me . . .

Do you remember what a pronoun is? A pronoun is a word used in place of a noun. There are subject pronouns and object pronouns.

I, he, she, we, and **they** are subject pronouns. **Me, him, her, us,** and **them** are object pronouns. **You** and **it** can be both subject and object pronouns.

Always use an object pronoun as the object of a preposition. After all, only an object can be an object! Look at these examples:

	EXAMPLES
WRONG	Keep this between you and I.
RIGHT	Keep this **between you and me.**
WRONG	Save some cake for Morgan and I.
RIGHT	Save some cake **for Morgan and me.**
WRONG	She showed her new puppy to he and Jane.
RIGHT	She showed her new puppy **to him and Jane.**

"Just between you and me, you're my best friend in the whole world." The preposition **between** is always followed by an object pronoun such as me.

Do some of the right examples sound funny? Never mind—they are correct! They may sound funny because so many people use the wrong pronoun after a preposition. It's a common mistake—and one you never have to make!

Fun with Prepositions

Here are some fun exercises. Write down your answers on a separate piece of paper.

Proverbs are wise sayings that teach a lesson. Fill in the right preposition to complete the proverbs below. You can use these prepositions: **at, by, in, of, on, over, to.**

1. Don't cross the bridge till you come _____ it.
2. A bird _____ the hand is worth two _____ the bush.
3. Birds _____ a feather flock together.
4. Charity begins _____ home.
5. You can't tell a book _____ its cover.
6. Don't cry _____ spilled milk.
7. The grass is always greener _____ the other side.
8. Life is just a bowl _____ cherries.

What do you think each proverb means?

See page 32 for the answers. Don't peek!

How to Learn More

IN THE LIBRARY

Atwood, Megan, and Sole Otero (illustrator). *Patrick and Paula Learn about Prepositions.* Chicago, IL: Norwood House Press, 2015.

Cleary, Brian P., and Brian Gable (illustrator). *Under, Over, By the Clover: What Is a Preposition?* Minneapolis, MN: Millbrook Press, 2014.

Meister, Cari, and Holli Conger (illustrator). *Who Is Up There? A Book about Prepositions.* Mankato, MN: Amicus, 2016.

Preciado, Tony, and Rhode Montijo (illustrator). *Super Grammar: Learn Grammar with Superheroes.* New York, NY: Scholastic, 2012.

ON THE WEB

Visit our website for links about prepositions:
childsworld.com/links

Note to Parents, Teachers, and Librarians: We routinely verify our web links to make sure they are safe and active sites. So encourage your readers to check them out!

Index

Answers

page 7

Preposition	Object	Introduces
1. with	toes	description
2. at	five o'clock	time
3. beside	lake	place
4. through	hoop	place

page 13

There are many possible answers.
Here are some suggestions:

1. The cat with the hat put his head on the bed.
2. My dog saw a frog with a rose on its nose.
3. A fish jumped into a dish and splashed its tail in the pail.
4. Jack has a yak with a sack on its back.

Answers to Fun with Prepositions

1. to
2. in, in
3. of
4. at
5. by
6. over
7. on
8. of